FOREIGN POLICY ASSOCIATION
Headline Series

No. 260 SEPTEMBER/OCTOBER 1982 $3.00

THE SOVIET ECONOMY
Past, Present and Future

by Franklyn D. Holzman

Cover design: Hersch Wartik; cover photo: Sven Simon

The Author

FRANKLYN D. HOLZMAN is professor of economics at Tufts University, adjunct professor at the Fletcher School of Law and Diplomacy, and a research associate at the Harvard Russian Research Center. He also taught at the University of Washington and has been visiting professor at Stanford, UCLA, Columbia and MIT. He has served as consultant to the UN Economic and Social Council, the Presidential Commission on Trade and Investment Policy, and the U.S. Departments of State, Treasury and Commerce. In 1977 he was president of the Association for Comparative Economic Studies. Professor Holzman received his Ph.D. from Harvard University and has written extensively on the Soviet economy.

The Foreign Policy Association

The Foreign Policy Association is a private, nonprofit, nonpartisan educational organization. Its purpose is to stimulate wider interest and more effective participation in, and greater understanding of, world affairs among American citizens. Among its activities is the continuous publication, dating from 1935, of the HEADLINE SERIES pamphlets. The authors of these pamphlets are responsible for factual accuracy and for the views expressed. FPA itself takes no position on issues of United States foreign policy.

HEADLINE SERIES (ISSN 0017-8780) is published five times a year, January, March, May, September and November, by the Foreign Policy Association, Inc., 205 Lexington Ave., New York, N.Y. 10016. Chairman, Leonard H. Marks; President, William E. Schaufele, Jr.; Editor, Nancy L. Hoepli; Associate Editor, Ann R. Monjo; Assistant Editor, Mary E. Stavrou. Subscription rates, $12.00 for 5 issues; $20.00 for 10 issues; $28.00 for 15 issues. Single copy price $3.00. Discount 25% on 10 to 99 copies; 30% on 100 to 499; 35% on 500 to 999; 40% on 1,000 or more. Payment must accompany order for $5 or less. Second-class postage paid at New York, N.Y. POSTMASTER: Send address changes to the Foreign Policy Association. **Composed and printed at Science Press, Ephrata, Pa.**

Library of Congress Catalog No. 82-84003
ISBN 0-87124-078-5

1

Introduction

Since the end of World War II, the major focus of U.S. foreign policy has been to contain the Soviet Union geographically, militarily, politically and economically in order to prevent the development and spread of communism. During the fifties and much of the sixties U.S. relations with the U.S.S.R. were locked in a "cold war." That war was abandoned for *détente* at the end of the sixties. By then the U.S.S.R. was approaching the United States in military strength and both countries, fearful of nuclear war, wanted to limit the arms race. Moreover, our allies in Western Europe were already implementing détente. By the late seventies, however, détente was beginning to lose its appeal, and the Soviet invasion of Afghanistan in December 1979 ended it for the Carter Administration. Soviet encouragement of the crack-down on Solidarity in Poland in 1981 further soured relations between the United States and the Soviet Union.

A preliminary and more technical version of this study was prepared for Evans Economics, Inc. and was circulated to its clients in Spring 1981 as part of a larger volume entitled International Outlook. *This version is published with their permission.*

COMPARATIVE SIZE AND ALLOCATION OF US AND SOVIET ECONOMIES

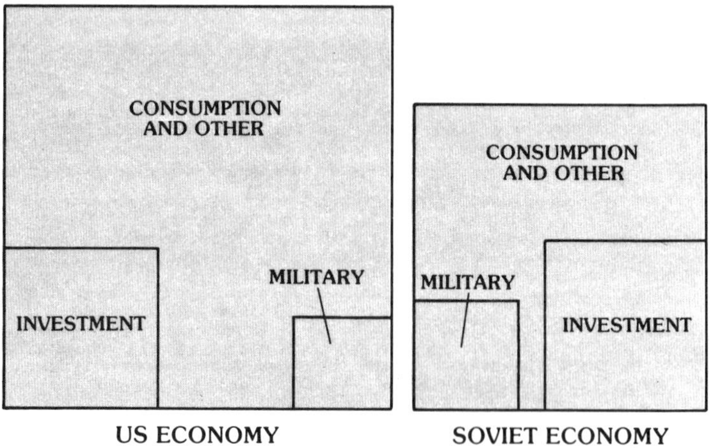

Department of Defense Annual Report to Congress FY 1983

Thoroughly disillusioned with the "illusion of détente," the Reagan Administration has sharply increased projected military expenditures and reduced high-technology and energy-related exports to the U.S.S.R. Both policies have run into opposition at home and abroad. Domestic critics fear nuclear war and are concerned by the drain on the civilian economy, especially on major social programs. Opposition in the North Atlantic Treaty Organization (NATO) is based partly on fear of war, partly on a reluctance to reduce economic ties with the U.S.S.R. and Eastern Europe. For West Europeans, these ties mean substantial supplies of raw materials, especially natural gas and petroleum, and an export market for many of their manufactured products. In 1981 and 1982 the United States tried unsuccessfully to pressure seven of its West European allies not to go ahead with the

Urengoi-Yamburg pipeline deal, which by the late 1980s would involve Soviet shipment of approximately $10 billion worth of natural gas annually from Siberia to Western Europe.

The Reagan Administration's economic policy toward the U.S.S.R. is predicated, in part, on the belief that the Soviet economy is in serious trouble and that Soviet policy can therefore be influenced by U.S. economic pressure and the prohibitive costs of an expanded arms race. The Soviet economy does indeed appear to be much less robust than it once was. The economy that Premier Nikita S. Khrushchev boasted in 1960 would "overtake and surpass the United States in 20 years" is, in fact, only a little closer to the American economy now than it was then. Indeed, it has grown so slowly over the past five years that it would probably need another century, at the present pace, to fulfill Khrushchev's prediction. And as the overall economy goes, so goes the consumer. After six decades of intensive economic development, the U.S.S.R. is still far behind the United States in quantity of consumption. The goods it does produce are shoddy, and long lines for the most elementary of essentials seem to have become permanent fixtures. At present, some goods are in such short supply that rationing is reported to have been introduced in a number of cities. To make matters worse, the Soviets have had four bad harvest years in a row necessitating vast quantities of food imports.

Paradoxically, this same political and economic system is supremely capable of producing large quantities of high-quality weapons and spacecraft, and many now claim that it has achieved military parity with the United States. Further, it is only fair to note that, despite its many problems, the Soviet economy has grown steadily and, until very recently, at a fairly respectable pace since the end of World War II. Moreover, it would be partisan not to mention that the economic performance of the United States, as well as most other major Western industrial nations, is also far below what it was during the first 25 years after World War II.

In order to put the U.S.S.R.'s current economic problems into perspective, it is useful to review the Soviet economy's track record. How fast did it grow? What specific problems confronted it? How successful have attempts at reform been? It is also important to look at the special configuration of problems facing the Soviets in the 1980s and at their likely courses of action. Such a survey will provide a basis for evaluating the wisdom of current U.S. economic policies toward the U.S.S.R.

Soviet Central Planning

But first it is necessary to understand how the Soviet economy works. Unlike Western capitalist countries, in which market forces largely determine how much of what gets produced, when and for whom, the Soviet Union operates under a system of central planning by direct controls. Every five years, the central planners at the State Planning Committee (or Gosplan) in Moscow draw up general guidelines to serve as a medium-term blueprint for the economy. Within this framework, detailed plans are drawn up each year that serve as a guide for most transactions. Annual plans may deviate from the five-year plans, and adjustments may even be made quarterly if the state of the economy so requires.

Planning so huge an economy is obviously an enormously complex task. The political leaders first set major goals for military spending, rates of consumption and investment, and so forth. The Gosplan, together with other economic organizations, then determines what the economy is to produce—everything from the number of apartment houses and aircraft carriers to the number of nails. Next, the Gosplan must calculate just how much raw material, equipment, labor and semifinished parts are needed to make each of these products. In light of the above, the committee sets production goals for virtually all Soviet enterprise, from Omsk to Tomsk and Minsk to Pinsk. Most enterprises are then presented with their supply or delivery plans: when and where to ship their products and when and from whom they can expect deliveries. Finally, a state committee periodically sets prices, approximately 10 million to 20 million of them. The complexity of setting that many prices is so great that, with minor exceptions, they remained unchanged between the price reform of

1967 and the reform introduced in 1982. Prices that remain fixed for so long do not, of course, reflect supply and demand and therefore cannot provide the authorities with accurate planning information.

The day-to-day supervision of the economy is the job of some 40 ministries in charge of specific industries or groups of industries. Subordinate to the ministries are the thousands of enterprises—since 1973 combined into so-called production associations—carrying out actual production. Each enterprise and production association is run by a state-appointed manager, whose major goal is to fulfill—or, if possible, overfulfill—his planned output quota. The manager's right-hand man is the *tolkach,* an expediter who hunts for scarce resources on the black market. His job is to make sure that his enterprise always has enough of what it needs to fulfill the plan. Failure of any enterprise to fulfill its plan means trouble for the rest. If, for example, enterprise A fails to achieve its output target, it will not be able to fulfill its commitment to enterprise B. In turn, enterprise B will fail to achieve its output target and be unable to supply enterprise C, and so on. The plant managers of A, B and C all stand to lose sizable bonuses unless the tolkach steps in and finds an alternative source of the missing product. Clearly, such a system is highly inefficient, and this explains why the tolkach is tolerated by authorities. Failure to meet an output target can cause bottlenecks that have repercussions several times more costly than the value of the original shortfall.

The manager also has other targets, such as profits, cost reduction, and labor productivity, but the bonus he gets for just fulfilling the plan, which amounts to 20–30 percent of base pay, leads him to concentrate on making sure he achieves his output target.

One major consequence of this system is the poor quality of most Soviet goods, excepting those produced for the military sector. As the major rewards are for quantity, plant managers have little incentive to strive for quality. Quality suffers further because managers do not compete for markets; they simply deliver according to plan. Moreover, because of overfull employment planning—i.e. planning for higher levels of output than are possible, given the available supplies of inputs—shortages and sellers' markets are widespread, and consumers have to make do with whatever they get.

Another important consequence is the resistance of plant managers to technological change. There are several reasons for this. Introducing new technology can so disrupt factory routine as to lead to a loss of bonuses for several months. Then, too, a change in technology often involves changes in supplies and suppliers, thereby disrupting the extensive networks of reliable sources of supply that managers and expediters work so hard to develop. Finally, if an enterprise does fulfill its quota more easily, thanks to better technology, the state usually responds with higher output targets, thus leaving the enterprise no better off than it was before.

In many ways, the Soviet direct-control model is similar to that employed by capitalist nations in time of war. The United States did not rely on markets during World War II to raise an army or to ensure that steel and many other essential materials were shifted from civilian to military use. Like the U.S.S.R. in peacetime, the United States in wartime had urgent goals that had to be achieved rapidly, and this led to widespread shortages of civilian goods, among other things. Although achieving priority goals and restructuring the economy by such means does get the job done, considerable losses usually accrue to the rest of the economy and to society in general. A look at the Soviet Union's economic development since 1928 brings this point home.

2

The Soviet Economy 1928-80

In 1928, the year the First Five-Year Plan was launched, the Soviet economy was some 30 to 50 years behind the advanced industrial nations of the West. Approximately 80 percent of the people still lived in rural areas; the population was poorly educated, and fewer than half of those over 18 years of age could either read or write. True, agriculture had recovered to pre-World War I levels thanks to the New Economic Policy (1921–27), which encouraged private production. But the price for keeping the peasants happy was an inability to mobilize resources for rapid industrial development. In turn, the lack of desirable consumer goods was beginning to affect agriculture negatively, as peasants, having little to buy, began to sell less of their output to the state. To make matters worse, the Communist party, whose strongholds were the cities, started seeing itself drowning in a sea of capitalist peasantry.

Enter Stalin. As Soviet Premier Joseph Stalin and his cohorts saw it, continued Communist domination required taming the peasantry. At the same time the survival of the Soviet Union as a

Communist country in a world of hostile capitalist nations seemed to make it essential to modernize and industrialize as rapidly as possible. Stalin concluded that investment had to be raised sharply; peasants had to be forced to deliver more of their grain to the state to feed the enlarged labor force; labor had to be transferred from rural to urban areas to run the new factories; and technology and equipment had to be imported and paid for with raw materials and food products, especially grain.

Grain for Export, Famine at Home

How was Stalin to accomplish these goals in the face of a hostile peasantry? His answer was collectivization. Private farming was rapidly abolished, the peasants were herded onto collective farms, and those who resisted were either shot or deported to Siberia. The peasants responded by slaughtering their animals and working less. But Stalin remained undaunted: as grain production plummeted, he increased state grain procurements and grain exports. The result was a massive famine that took the lives of many peasants. The peasants who survived famine, liquidation and deportation to Siberia became pliant subjects of Stalin's state.

Workers, meanwhile, though enjoying a slightly higher standard of living than the peasants, were also subject to strict totalitarian controls. Minor infractions of labor discipline were often punished severely and were sometimes regarded as attempts at sabotage. All in all, the standard of living of the entire population was lower in 1940 than it had been in 1928, or even 1913. In statistical terms, however, the Soviet economy was growing by leaps and bounds as a result of the rapid expansion in extraction of raw materials (iron ore, coal, oil, etc.) and production of machinery and equipment. In the period of the first two five-year plans, 1928–37, gross national product (GNP) grew annually by 8 to 9 percent, while industrial production grew by almost 15 percent. Labor was also better trained. The percentage of illiterates declined from 56 percent in 1926 to 20 percent by 1939; the number of persons completing seven grades of school increased from 6 million to 14 million a year; and the number of university graduates rose from about one-half million to over a million.

Foreign trade was also harnessed to the needs of industrialization. The volume of imports increased by 60 percent between 1929 and 1931, but by the latter date only 5 percent of imports were consumer goods. The other 95 percent were machinery, equipment and technology necessary to the industrialization drive.

Growth slowed significantly between 1938 and 1941, however. Preparations for war had begun, and the economy was disrupted by the secret-police terror, political trials (1936–38) and imprisonment of millions of people, many who had held important management positions, in concentration camps.

Postwar Recovery

Then came World War II. The U.S.S.R. suffered enormous physical devastation and at least 20 million dead. But recovery was rapid. Within four or five years, industrial output had regained prewar levels. In the 1950s, GNP grew by about 6 percent and industrial production by 10 percent per annum. Moreover, Soviet agricultural output, in comparison with the no-growth record of the 1930s, rose annually by about 5 percent. Per capita household consumption grew at almost the same rate.

Very important to the Soviet Union's rapid economic growth was the degree to which the educational system was geared to economic needs. By 1959 roughly 60 million working-age persons had received more than a seventh-grade education, in contrast with only 14 million in 1939. By 1958 the U.S.S.R. had 6.7 university enrollments per 1,000 population, more than Germany, France and the United Kingdom, but less than Japan and the United States. Perhaps most significantly, in the three decades ending in 1959, the U.S.S.R. graduated 2.4 million engineers, doctors, agronomists and science majors from institutions of higher learning in contrast with 1.7 million for the United States. The United States, on the other hand, graduated 5.2 million in the humanities, social sciences and other nontechnical disciplines, as opposed to 1.8 million for the U.S.S.R., an indication of the more liberal goals of our society.

Exit Stalin

The major event of the 1950s was political—Stalin's death in 1953. His death was followed by a considerable reduction in the much-hated secret-police terror. His successors, Georgi Malenkov and Khrushchev, also quickly took measures to improve the standard of living, both out of concern for the harsh lot of the population and in order to generate support for their leadership. In contrast with Stalin, who had exploited the peasants mercilessly, his successors paid them higher wages so as to encourage greater effort and allowed collective farms to own their farm machinery. A major housing construction effort was also launched.

The most dramatic development in agriculture was Khrushchev's "virgin lands" program. In a monumental effort to raise agricultural output precipitously, 100 million acres of marginal land in western Siberia and Kazakhstan were put into cultivation over a period of two to three years. While the productivity of these areas was low and many considered the project far too costly, grain output was increased.

By the second half of the 1950s, however, Soviet economic performance had begun to decline. This trend continued through the first half of the 1960s and was reflected in a significant drop in the rate of growth of the GNP as a whole. Industry grew at half the rate achieved in the 1930s, and at only 60 percent of the 1951–55 rate; growth in per capita consumption declined by close to a third of the 1951–55 rate. The economic performance was still respectable, of course, but the downward trend no doubt caused considerable concern.

That all was not well with the Soviet economic juggernaut was brought dramatically to the attention of the world by Khrushchev's decision in September 1957 not to complete the Sixth Five-Year Plan (1956–60) and to replace it with a Seven-Year Plan running from 1959 through 1965. But the severity of the

Soviets' economic problems became especially clear from the succession of reforms that followed Khrushchev's ouster and that continue to this day.

Behind the Economic Slowdown

Obviously, something was wrong with the Soviet economy, but what? And what could be done about it? There is no single or simple answer to the first question, but several factors do stand out.

Clearly the central planning system developed by Stalin for the 1930s was no longer appropriate for the 1950s and beyond. Stalin's model was applicable to an underdeveloped economy that could be made to grow "extensively" just by rapidly mobilizing large quantities of resources, such as labor, capital, raw materials, etc. The principle was simple. If there were unemployed workers, put them to work in the mines and factories. If there were not enough factories, raise the rate of investment and build more. If there were too few workers in industry and too many in agriculture, shift the excess out of agriculture and into industry. If workers were unqualified for the new jobs, train them. Government controls could effectively foster extensive growth of this kind in an underdeveloped economy because the job primarily involved gross coordination of the allocation of labor and resources.

Of course, the direct controls exercised by planners were blunt instruments. So, for example, many of the peasants drafted wholesale into factories were incompetent and unwilling to operate industrial machinery; planners determining shoe output in their Moscow offices often produced the wrong combination of sizes and styles; bureaucrats far away were less competent than collective-farm managers to decide which farms were best suited for which crops. Initially, such inefficiencies were tolerable. Once rapid mobilization and restructuring of resources had been achieved, however, they became burdensome. Even more serious was the fact that the sources of extensive growth were exhaustible. Once full employment had been achieved, the labor force had been educated, low-productivity agriculture had been reduced in size, and the economy had been provided with a sizable capital stock through massive investment, additional huge quantitative inputs became physically impossible.

What is the alternative to extensive growth? The answer is "intensive" growth—improving the quality, instead of increasing the quantity, of the factors of production. Intensive growth primarily involves raising the technological level of the capital stock: for example, modernizing machinery, improving the quality of tools, replacing mechanical computers with electronic computers, etc. In and of itself, the shift from extensive to intensive growth is both costly and time-consuming, but when confronted with a central planning system resistant to technological innovation and to new ways of doing things, the transition to intensiveness becomes even more difficult. Nonetheless, as the Soviets now realize, it is imperative if their economy is to grow.

Other factors responsible for Soviet economic troubles need to be mentioned. Central planning of the Soviet economy in the 1930s and 1950s, while complex, was nevertheless much simpler than in later years. The priorities and needs in those days were clear-cut: produce more steel, coal, tractors, shoes, radios and the like. As the economy developed and basic needs were taken care of, the choices both in production and consumption became more varied and complicated. This multiplied on a grand scale the complexity of the problems facing central planners. They were further handicapped by the absence of a rational price system upon which to base their economic decisions.

The rise in the military's share of the GNP—from about 5 percent over the 1928–37 period to 13 percent in the 1950s—also had negative spin-offs on the rest of the economy. Military research and development siphoned from the civilian economy many of its best scientists and engineers and reduced the rate at which the Soviets were able to develop new civilian technology for raising productivity and increasing growth.

Despite 20 years of experience with central planning, the Soviet authorities had not learned that overfull employment planning—planning to produce more output than is physically possible given the resources—was bound to have an adverse impact on economic performance. This manifested itself in various ways. Managers, unable to produce as much as planned, were unable to fulfill scheduled delivery to other enterprises or to final consumers. In the former case, this led to bottlenecks and further underfulfillment of targets, not to mention the need for the tolkach and black markets; in the latter case, it led to consumers faced with shortages, long lines at stores, dissatisfaction and low morale. Another problem: given pervasive shortages, managers were typically faced with sellers' markets—markets in which they could sell anything they produced. This left them with little incentive to produce quality goods or to please customers. Still another problem, one due both to overfull employment planning and to the fact that interest costs had never been a serious constraint on investment in Communist countries, was that more new investment projects had been started each year than could be finished as planned. As the years passed, the number of unfinished projects increased, and the amount of output resulting from each ruble of new investment had correspondingly declined.

The Economic Reforms of 1957 and 1965

What, then, was to be done about the economy? Stalin's successors responded with a series of reforms. The first was introduced in 1957 by Khrushchev, as much for political as for economic reasons. In essence, it changed the administrative structure of the economy and the government by replacing the 30-odd industrial ministries with 105 regional economic councils (*sovnarkhozy*). Politically, the reorganization enabled Khrushchev to replace a number of powerful ministers with regional supporters. Economically, the reform was designed to eliminate three problems that had developed in response to the uncertainties of getting deliveries and services under the supply-planning system. First, ministries were duplicating one another's efforts by building their own auxiliary plants so as not to have to depend on other ministries for parts, repairs and the like. Second, ministries facing difficulties getting certain supplies from other ministries were shipping such supplies from distant enterprises under their own jurisdiction, a practice that overloaded the transportation system. Finally, it was hoped that the reform would eliminate the need for the tolkach or fixer.

In fact, the reform was administrative, not economic, and it merely addressed the symptoms rather than the disease. The need to eliminate uncertainty by becoming self-sufficient remained. Although self-sufficiency was now practiced by regions rather than ministries, deliveries to enterprises were as irregular as ever, and the tolkach did not disappear. Instead of going to Moscow, he was more likely to go to the capital city of the region.

The experiment with regions was less than a success and was abandoned, and in 1965 ministries were restored by the so-called Kosygin reforms. These reforms, named for Alexei Kosygin (premier, 1964–80), attempted to eliminate other defects of central planning by improving the pricing mechanism, by introducing some decentralization and by getting away from purely quantitative goals and the deterioration of quality that these encouraged. Interest and rent charges were to be included in price, but there was no reason to believe that these charges approximated their market values. Sales and profits were introduced as enterprise goals, but without rational prices, profits made little sense. Since bonuses for meeting the profit target continued to be much less than those for meeting the sales target, enthusiasm for the former never caught on. Moreover, as long as the Soviets continued to ration inputs and outputs according to the plan, they could not shift to profit incentives since profit-motivated enterprises well might not produce the quantities required. Finally, plant managers were supposed to have more power to use their profits or bank loans to invest in projects not specified in the plan, and to hire and fire employees. These powers, however, turned out to be difficult to implement as the supplies needed for unspecified investments were usually not to be had unless already centrally planned, and firing workers was next to impossible because de facto job tenure was so widespread.

The Kosygin reforms had almost no long-term impact on the Soviet economy. Nevertheless, the Soviet performance in the late

1960s did improve in comparison with the downturn of the early 1960s. Things had to get better after the particularly anarchic situation caused by Khrushchev's tinkering with and tailoring of the system. The second half of the 1960s may also have benefited from the rapid expansion of trade, especially with Western Europe.

Slowdown in the 1970s

The 1970s witnessed several disturbing trends in the Soviet economy. To begin with, they marked a turning point in the Soviet battle with agriculture. The U.S.S.R. had traditionally been able to supply its own grain needs, as well as meet the import requirements of its East European allies. During the 1970s, however, reliance on grain imports from the West became what appears to be a permanent part of the Soviet foreign trade picture (see pages 18 and 19).

The inability of the Soviets to achieve self-sufficiency in agriculture has not been for lack of trying. During the Ninth Five-Year Plan (1971–75), productive investment in agriculture grew at an annual rate of more than 9.5 percent, faster than in any other sector, and amounted to about 20 percent of total investment over the five-year period. If funds spent for such nonproductive purposes as rural housing are included, agriculture's direct share of investment rises to 26 percent. If investment in supportive industries (e.g. fertilizer) is also included, agriculture's total share for the five years amounts to over 34 percent, or almost five times the comparable U.S. share. Nevertheless, Soviet agriculture has continued to stagnate.

Another negative trend in the seventies was the rising cost of raw materials. In the case of petroleum, this was due to the low quality of remaining reserves and to the fact that many of them were located in remote Siberia, far from centers of use and in extremely inhospitable areas where exploitation was expensive. In 1979, for example, oil and gas were being transported three times as far as in 1960, and coal 25 percent farther.

The one bright spot in the economic picture of the 1970s was

Soviet Grain Output

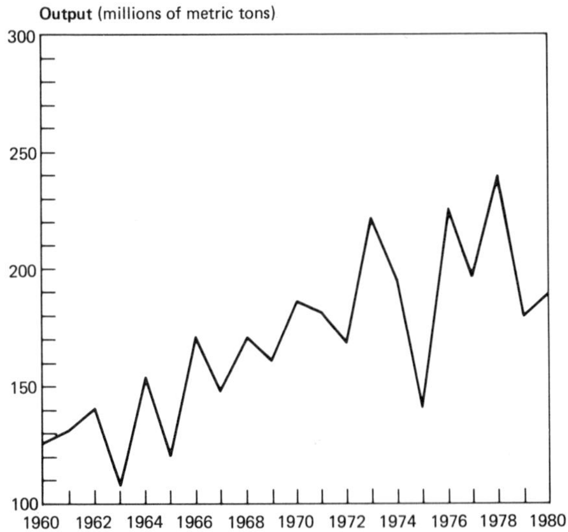

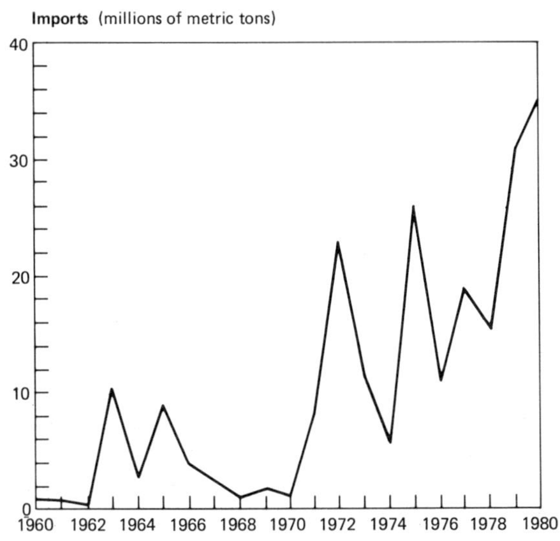

and Gross Imports, 1960–80

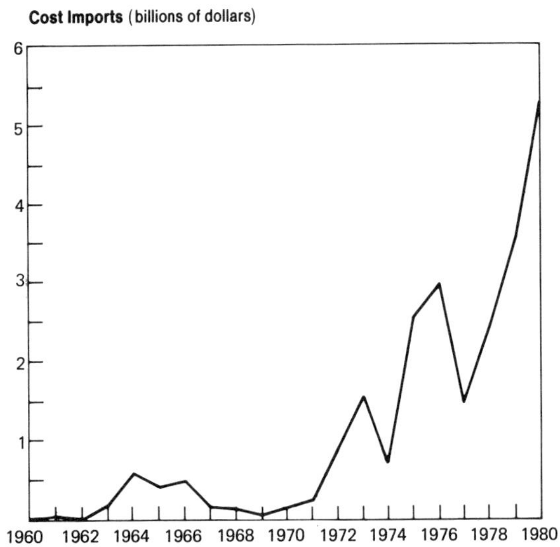

Source: Centrally Planned Economies Service, Wharton Econometric Forecasting Associates.

The figures presented for imports take no account of the fact that the Soviets regularly export grains to Eastern Europe. With the possible exceptions of 1963 and 1965, grain exports exceeded grain imports in the 1960s. Since 1971, the Soviets have been a net importer of grain. The rising cost of imports partly reflects rising prices of grain.

the rapid increase in international trade (particularly with the West), thanks to which the U.S.S.R. was able to import grain, machinery, equipment and new technology (see Table 1). Very important in this regard was the sharp rise in the price of oil after 1973, which changed the entire constellation of world prices and brought the Soviets large windfall gains from sales of petroleum, gas, gold and arms. Rough estimates suggest that the Soviets gained more than $15 billion from improved terms of trade from 1971 to 1977, plus an additional $8 billion because of higher gold prices in 1971–79. Without these gains, either their foreign debt would have been at least twice as high or imports from the West would have been more restrained.

Table 1
U.S.S.R.: Selected Hard Currency Exports, Gold Sales, and Imports
(in millions of current U.S. dollars)

Since most Soviet trade is not in hard currency (a currency that is freely convertible into the currency of other countries, e.g. the dollar, mark, franc, yen, etc.) but represents exchanges within the Soviet bloc, the total hard currency exports and imports represent less than one third of total exports and imports. The rapid rise in value of trade between 1972 and 1978 is due, to a considerable extent, to rising prices. The failure of exports to increase in 1975 reflects the Western recession; and the leveling off of imports after 1975 reflects an effort to control the rise in debt to the West.

	1972	1974	1976	1978	1980
Total exports	2,801	7,470	9,721	13,157	23,792
of which:					
machinery and equipment	225	340	657	1,209	—
petroleum and petroleum products	556	2,548	4,514	5,716	—
natural gas	23	86	347	1,063	—
wood and wood products	403	1,002	852	975	—
Sales of gold	380	1,178	1,369	2,522	800
Total imports	4,157	8,448	15,316	16,951	26,247
of which:					
machinery and equipment	1,282	2,334	5,074	5,969	—
rolled ferrous metals (including pipe)	489	1,892	2,251	2,480	—
food (including grain)	981	1,001	3,401	3,175	5,276[a]

[a]Cost of grain imports alone (Wharton Econometric Forecasting Associates).

Sources: Gold sales and 1980 data are from CIA, *Handbook of Economic Statistics*, various years. Other figures are from Paul G. Ericson and Ronald S. Miller, "Soviet Foreign Economic Behavior: A Balance of Payments Perspective," in *Soviet Economy in a Time of Change, II*, Joint Economic Committee, U.S. Congress, Washington, D.C., USGPO, 1979, pp. 241-42.

Economic Reforms in the 1970s

Two economic reforms were undertaken in the 1970s, the first in 1973, which by 1980 was half-completed, the second in 1979. The 1973 reform, known as the Production Association Reform, had two effects. It reduced the importance of the enterprise as the fundamental economic unit by integrating large numbers of related enterprises into a production association. By taking power away from enterprises and giving it to the production association, the authorities had, in effect, given up on decentralization as a means of getting good performances out of enterprises. Perhaps more important, the reform assigned each of the research and development institutes, which formerly served hundreds of enterprises in an industry, to a production association. This side of the reform represented an attempt to bring together the suppliers and users of new technology and thereby encourage practical innovation and its use. It also indicated that the central planners recognized that they had left the extensive phase of economic growth and must take measures to encourage intensive growth. Presumably, once a new technology was made practical, the production associations would be in a position to push the enterprises into adopting it.

The 1979 reform placed still greater emphasis on planning and tried to facilitate technological change. Planning was much more detailed, and long-range planning (for five and ten years) was given considerably greater weight than previously, relative to short-range annual planning. Long-range planning makes it possible, of course, to build projected technological change into the plans.

While both reforms of the 1970s were designed to meet current Soviet economic problems, there is no evidence yet that either has had a discernible impact on performance. Soviet economic performance has continued to deteriorate. Growth of GNP declined to little more than 1 percent per year in 1979 and 1980 (see graph, page 22). Growth of industrial production declined to about 3 percent in the second half of the 1970s. The growth of agricultural output also fell, ending up in the 1970s with a growth rate of about 2 percent per annum (see page 31). Finally, growth in per capita household consumption declined to 2.6 percent per annum in the second half of the 1970s.

Table 2
U.S.S.R.: Growth in Per Capita Consumption, 1951-80
(average annual rates of growth in percentages)

Growth in per capita consumption over the postwar period is very impressive, although it has been declining, mirroring the gradual drop in growth of GNP.

	1951-55	1956-60	1961-65	1966-70	1971-75	1976-80
Total consumption	5.3	4.2	3.7	5.3	3.6	2.6

Source: CIA, *Handbook of Economic Statistics*, 1981, p. 56.

U.S.S.R.: Growth of Gross National Product[1] by Sector of Origin, 1971–80

(average annual percentage change)

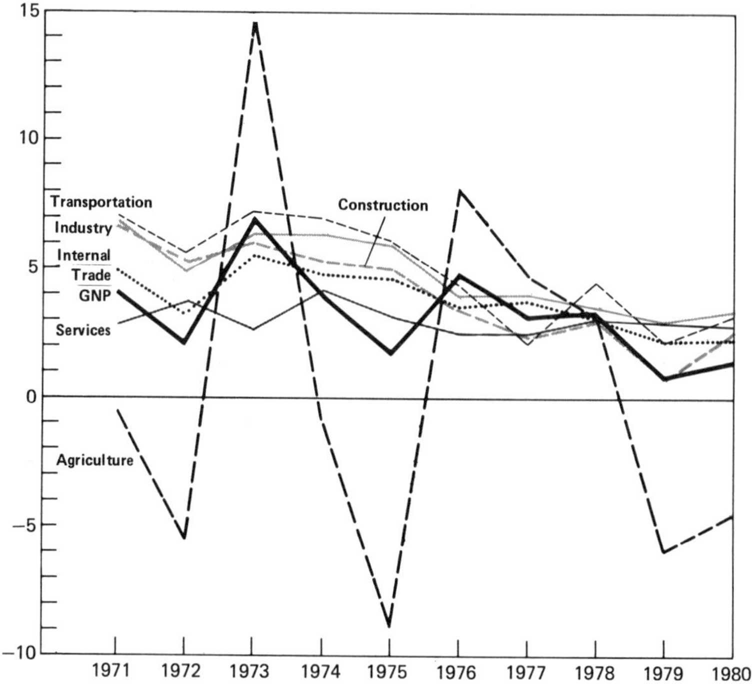

[1]Calculated at factor costs.

Sources: For 1971-74, CIA, *The Soviet Economy in 1978–79 and Prospects for 1980,* p. 25; for 1975–80, CIA, *Handbook,* 1981, p. 57.

The chart shows that over the decade, 1971–80, growth in GNP is lower in every year, except 1973, than the average five-year growth rates between 1950 and 1970 depicted in Table 5, page 49. The year 1973 is exceptional because of the effect of excellent weather on agricultural output. Large agricultural output also improves the performances of industry, transportation and internal trade, as the figures for 1973 show; analogously, poor crops depress GNP directly and depress these other three sectors as well, although the potential drop in internal trade may be prevented by large imports of food, as demonstrated in chart on page 18.

While these figures capture much of the essence of the problem, they do not tell the whole story. The economic data cast no light on the low and declining levels of physical and mental health in the U.S.S.R., as evidenced by increases in alcoholism, abortions and infant mortality, and in the recent decline in male life expectancy. Nor do they say much about the low quality of consumer products, the frequent unavailability of some goods—such as soap, meat, toilet paper or shoes—or the necessity of standing in line for hours in order to buy scarce goods. In his book *The Russians,* Hedrick Smith, chief Washington correspondent of *The New York Times,* has captured the manic quality of surviving as a consumer in the U.S.S.R. "Personally," he writes, "I have known of people who stood in line 90 minutes to buy four pineapples, three hours for a two-minute roller coaster ride, three and a half hours to buy three large heads of cabbage . . . 18 hours to sign up to purchase a rug at some later date, all through a freezing December night to register on a list for buying a car. . . ."

3

Economic Balance Sheet in the 1980s

As the U.S.S.R. moves into the 1980s, the big questions are whether its economic performance will continue to deteriorate, and, if so, how that will affect not only the Soviet citizenry but the Soviet military posture and East-West relations. Regardless of the answer, the U.S.S.R. will have to make difficult decisions concerning the allocation of its scarce resources to major sectors—consumption, investment and the military. To some extent, these decisions will be constrained by noneconomic factors, such as NATO military policies, or the extent to which the Soviet population is willing to sit back silently while its economic expectations and aspirations go unrealized. Overall performance in the 1980s will also be conditioned by trends or potential trends in several areas.

POPULATION TRENDS

One of the major problems facing the U.S.S.R. is a shift in the size and structure of its population. First of all, the natural increase in population has fallen from more than 17 per 1,000

Table 3
U.S.S.R.: Population of Working Age[1]
(million persons midyear)

Total population of working age changes annually by the amount of the annual increment (column 2). The annual increment is enlarged each year by the number of 16-year-olds entering the labor force and is decreased by workers' dying plus those retiring (women at age 55 and men at 60). The numbers of deaths and departures have increased as the work force has aged. The decline in entrants between 1955 and 1960 and negative increment in 1960 are due to the sharp drop in births during the 1941–45 war years. This same birth deficit is partly responsible for the projected decline in entrants and increments in the mid-1980s. The declining birthrate in general also contributes to the small annual increments projected for the mid-1980s.

	Total	Annual Increments	Entrants (16-year-olds)	Deaths	Departures (55/60-year-olds)
1955	114.7	2.7	4.7	0.4	1.6
1960	119.5	−0.1	1.9	0.2	1.8
1965	124.1	1.5	4.1	0.5	2.1
1970	131.7	1.7	4.5	0.6	2.2
1975	144.4	2.7	5.1	0.5	1.9
1980	155.8	1.6	4.5	0.5	2.4
1985	159.2	0.4	4.0	0.7	2.9
1990	161.9	0.7	4.4	0.7	3.0

[1]Males age 16–59, females age 16–54.

Source: U.S. Department of Commerce, Bureau of Economic Analysis, September 1976. Taken from: CIA, *USSR: Some Implications of Demographic Trends for Economic Policies,* January 1977, p. 4. 1955-75, actual data; 1980–90, projection.

in the period 1950-60 to 9 in 1980 and is expected to drop still further to 7.5 by 1990. More important, the population itself is aging—with ever larger proportions of older persons and ever smaller proportions of women of child-bearing age. In addition, family size is growing smaller. What this means for the economy is a steady decline in the rate of growth of the labor force (see Table 3). Thus, for example, the number of persons becoming 16 years of age reached a peak of 5.2 million in 1977. Since then it has been declining and is expected to be 4 million by 1984. Greatly compounding the problem is the fact that a regional disequilibrium is developing between supply and demand. Most Soviet-projected investment is scheduled for European Russia or Siberia, where the natural increase in population is low—around 6 per 1,000. Much of the increase in population and labor force in the future will come from the Transcaucasian republics, Kazakhstan and the other Central Asian republics, with natural increases of 18, 19 and 30 per 1,000, respectively. The Soviet planners' dilemma is unenviable: on the one hand, the Islamic peoples of these regions are known for their unwillingness to leave their homelands; on the other, the planners are loathe to bring industry to a region where anti-Soviet feeling is strong and many of the people are not even competent speakers of Russian.

Another constraint on Soviet economic performance is the fact that labor's effectiveness on the job depends greatly on the morale and health of the population. There is considerable evidence that in both respects Soviet conditions have deteriorated. For example, while infant mortality rates had declined steadily after World War II, they rose abruptly in the early 1970s—from 22.9 deaths per 1,000 in 1971 to an estimated 31.1 in 1976. This was probably due to a number of factors, one of which seems to be the very large number of abortions (an average of six) Soviet women have in their lifetimes.

Another unexpected demographic development has been the decline in life expectancy, especially of working-age males, from 66 years in 1965-66 to an estimated 62-63 years a decade later. The statistical decline can, in part, be attributed to the rise in infant mortality. A major cause, however, is the much publicized increase in alcoholism and related problems such as industrial and traffic accidents. While total Soviet consumption of alcohol is not much greater than that in some other nations, most of it, in contrast with other nations, is of hard liquor rather than of wines and beers. In 1976, for example, 68.6 percent of total Soviet expenditures on alcoholic beverages was spent for hard liquor, in contrast with 26.3 percent in the United States and 13.8 percent in France. Apparently the number of deaths in the U.S.S.R. from acute alcoholism is many times higher than in other nations.

Solutions to the Labor Shortage

How can Soviet planners increase labor's input into the economy in the 1980s? There are several possibilities, some of which have already been tapped. The authorities have made it legal for workers to delay retirement—previously mandatory at 55 for women and at 60 for men. A considerable number of pensioners have already taken advantage of this opportunity to supplement their incomes, mostly on a part-time basis. The number of retirees willing to return to work, however, is limited. One reason may be that the shortage and poor quality of consumer goods hardly make it worthwhile. If worse comes to worst, the authorities may eventually force elderly people to remain in the labor force by raising the minimum retirement age—but at the present level of dissatisfaction, such a step is probably not politically feasible.

The authorities can also try to put the voluntarily unemployed such as housewives or sickly persons to work. Their contribution, however, would at most be marginal, since they constitute only 12 percent of the potential labor force, possibly the lowest percentage in the world. Moreover, because of the unavailability of consumer goods, the voluntarily unemployed are unlikely to have a strong incentive to work.

Another possibility would be to lengthen the work week. However, since this could not be achieved on a voluntary basis, it seems even less politically palatable than the two previous options.

If labor could be more rationally allocated throughout the economy, the effect on productivity would be equivalent to that of adding millions of workers to the labor force. Some feeble attempts have already been made in this direction. However, as in many other nations, it is almost impossible, for institutional reasons, to fire or relocate workers. In any event, without radical economic reform, very little change in this area can be expected.

Finally, a potentially important source of additional civilian labor is the Soviet armed forces, which number approximately 4.5 million men. A sharp reduction in international tensions would allow the Soviets to divert these men into productive work. In addition, there are probably more than a million civilians working in military research and development and other projects, some of whom could also be reassigned. Conceivably, these possibilities would provide the Soviets with a motive for détente and arms control.

MILITARY EXPENDITURES

What may make arms control particularly attractive to the U.S.S.R. is that the current arms race with the United States carries a very high price tag. Whereas military expenditures represent 5 to 6 percent of the GNP of the United States, according to the Central Intelligence Agency (CIA) they amount to 12 to 14 percent of Soviet GNP. It is difficult to determine the accuracy of the latter figures since the CIA provides almost no information with which to check its figures. The Rand Corporation, a California-based "think tank," subscribes to the CIA data but some experts consider it, if anything, a little high, others a little low.

The CIA estimate of current Soviet military expenditures is, in this author's view, misleading. The CIA claims that the U.S.S.R. has been outspending the United States since 1971—and by increasing amounts every year. At present, according to the CIA, Soviet military expenditures are 50 percent greater than those of the United States. Moreover, between 1971 and 1980 the Soviets are said to have outspent the United States by $420 billion in current prices. These data presumably explain how the Russians were able to catch up with, even overtake, the United States militarily. This interpretation, accepted by the Carter and Reagan Administrations, is one of the considerations in current plans to step up U.S. defense spending.

Those who differ with the CIA estimates consider them flawed in several respects, each of which leads to an overestimation of Soviet defense expenditures. A most important flaw is that the CIA normally compares the two nations' expenditures in dollar prices. Dollar prices exaggerate Soviet military spending by valuing the U.S.S.R.'s 4.5-million-man army at an average of close to $20,000 per man. While a dollar comparison of military expenditures has the Soviets outspending the United States by 50 percent, a reliable ruble comparison would probably put the two nations closer to parity. Earlier in the seventies the United States was undoubtedly outspending, in ruble prices, the U.S.S.R.

The least-biased method of comparing the military expenditures—and all other expenditures—of the two nations is to measure them in both dollars and rubles, with these two figures representing the outer limits within which the actual amount must fall. Usually, in order to represent the spending comparison as a single figure, an average of the dollar and ruble figures—or geometric mean—is used. This is, in fact, the method used by the CIA in virtually all of its other comparisons of spending by the United States and the Soviet Union. The geometric mean would, in this writer's view, probably put the Russians somewhat ahead of the United States currently, but perhaps behind over the course of the past decade.

Of course, the Reagan Administration's plans to step up military expenditures are based only in part on the CIA's military spending comparisons. In addition, the U.S.S.R.'s arms buildup, its growth in sophisticated weaponry, the size of Warsaw Pact armed forces in Europe, the invasion of Afghanistan in 1979, subversive activities in third-world nations, and involvement in the Polish crisis of 1980-81 all create legitimate fears among U.S. policy-makers and provide an understandable, if not necessarily correct, basis for the actions being advanced by the Administration. Nonetheless, there are many people in this country and in allied nations who are less alarmed than the Administraiion by the Soviet military posture and oppose the scale of the proposed U.S. defense expenditures.

The Soviet Perspective

How the U.S.S.R. will respond to the U.S. military buildup will depend, of course, not on how the United States perceives the military balance but on how Soviet leaders perceive it—and what it implies to them about U.S. intentions. The Soviets are probably less sanguine about their capabilities than the U.S. Administration seems to think they are. First, they undoubtedly take a "ruble's-eye view" of the world. In ruble prices, the more technologically advanced U.S. arsenal of weapons is extremely costly, and U.S. military expenditures appear very high.

Moreover, the Soviets do not direct all of their military expenditures at countering the United States. They maintain close to 1 million troops on their 4,000-mile border with China, and, according to former Secretary of Defense Harold Brown, "have felt obliged to allocate up to 20 percent of their total defense effort to the Far East and People's Republic of China." If 15 percent of Soviet defense expenditures in China is assumed to be wasted in terms of having no impact on the East-West conflict, then the CIA's current spending gap would decline from 50 to 27.5 percent and the decade spending gap would be reduced by at least $250 billion, from $420 billion to $170 billion.

Finally, the Soviets also assign great military importance to the West European military-industrial powers. Although the Soviets could presumably count on the assistance of their Warsaw Pact allies in the event of a conflict in Europe, that thought is less consoling than it seems. The East Europeans, and especially the Poles, are probably not the most reliable of allies, and they are far weaker militarily than the West Europeans. In 1980, for example, the West Europeans outspent them on defense, $95 billion compared with $17 billion. In fact, in the period 1971–80, NATO's total military expenditures were more than $250 billion greater than those of the Warsaw Pact countries.

The above figures do not tell the whole story, of course, but they do suggest something of how the Soviets view the military situation. Under such circumstances, it is highly probable that a U.S. military buildup will simply provoke a Soviet military buildup. The same thinking that has led the Reagan Administration to increase its military spending will also lead the Soviet leaders to increase theirs, though the difficulties involved are legion. A military buildup would aggravate Soviet domestic economic problems by reducing investment for civilian purposes, diverting skilled labor and research and development from civilian to military tasks, and perhaps reducing the flow of young unskilled and semiskilled workers into the already tight civilian labor force. All of these changes would slow the growth rate and reduce the amount of goods available for households. Even so, national security is almost sure to take precedence over economic growth in the future, as it has in the past.

AGRICULTURE

To a very considerable degree Soviet economic growth is dependent on agriculture, which contributes 15 to 20 percent of the GNP. Moreover, good and bad years in agriculture have a large impact on other sectors, especially on trade but also on industry and transportation. In other words, how goes agriculture, so goes the Soviet economy (see page 22).

The problem is that Soviet agricultural performance is erratic: it is excessively dependent on changes in temperature and rainfall. Moreover, although agricultural output has been growing, the growth rate has been declining despite very large capital investments. Investments are negated in part by a decline in the quantity and quality of agricultural labor (young people and males depart, leaving elderly women behind on the farms), difficulties in meeting fertilizer goals and the fact that additional applications of fertilizer meet with diminishing returns, and the continuation of unusually large crop losses during and after harvesting. The following figures provide dramatic evidence of the downward trend in growth of agricultural output.

	1951-60	1961-70	1971-77
Annual Average Growth (in percent):			
Output	4.8	3.0	2.0
Inputs	2.7	2.1	1.6
Total Productivity	2.1	1.0	.4

Source: Douglas B. Diamond and W. Lee Davis, "Comparative Growth in Output and Productivity in U.S. and U.S.S.R. Agriculture," in *Soviet Economy in a Time of Change, II,* Joint Economic Committee, U.S. Congress, Washington, D.C., USGPO, 1979, p. 32.

The estimates in this table suggest that the decline in growth of output has been due to a decline both in the growth of inputs (labor, capital and land) and in productivity. In the period

UN
SOCI
EUROPE
NORWAY
SWEDEN
ESTONIAN S.S.R.
Baltic Sea
FINLAND
Murmansk
KARELIA
NOVAYA ZEMLYA
MOLDAVIAN S.S.R.
LITH. S.S.R.
LATVIAN S.S.R.
Leningrad
Archangel
BELORUSSIAN S.S.R.
UKRAINIAN S.S.R.
Kiev
Moscow
Volga
Gorki
RUSSIAN SOVIET
KOMI
URAL MOUNTAINS
Ob
TYUMEN
Black Sea
CHUVASH
MARI
UDMURT
Don
TATAR
Volgograd
BASHKIR
Sverdlovsk
Tobolsk
Irtysh
GEORGIAN S.S.R.
KALMYK
Ural
TURKEY
Caspian Sea
GUREV
AKTYUBINSK
Omsk
KAZAKH S.S.R.
Aral Sea
AKMOLINSK
KUZN BAS
ARMENIAN S.S.R.
AZERBAIDZHAN S.S.R.
TURKMEN S.S.R.
UZBEK S.S.R.
KARAGANDA
SEMIPALATINSK
ALMA ATA
IRAN
KIRGIZ S.S.R.
TADZHIK S.S.R.
AFGHAN.
PAKIS.
C
MILES
0
400
800

Current History, Inc.

1971–77 the decline in growth of inputs was due to an unusually rapid exodus of agricultural workers as well as to a slowdown in the rate of increase of fertilizer supply. In addition to other factors, the decline in total productivity in 1971–77 reflected the uncommonly bad weather over this period.

Unfortunately for the Soviets, bad weather will probably continue to plague their agriculture for some time to come. According to CIA climatologists, there appears to be a weather cycle in the U.S.S.R. and the disastrous crop of 1975 represented the beginning of a new downturn in the cycle. The CIA has used weather projections to predict grain shortfalls through 1985. If these predictions prove true, imports of grain will continue to be very large (assuming that the Soviets import all that they need), and the drain on hard currency reserves will be heavy as it has been over the recent past (see pages 19 and 20). To the extent that grain imports are not adequate to meet domestic needs, the cost of meat imports will also rise.

Meat with the Potatoes

Perhaps the most important subgoal of Soviet agriculture is the target for meat consumption. Per capita meat consumption in the U.S.S.R. has been significantly below that of most other East European nations and about 15 years behind that of Poland. Not surprisingly, increasing meat consumption has become one of the centerpieces of the regime's promise to the consumer of a better life. Raising the level of meat output, however, places great demands on Soviet agriculture for several reasons. First, it takes many kilograms of feed to generate a kilogram of meat; under Soviet conditions, the ratios are roughly 13 to 1 for beef, 9 to 1 for pork, and 6 to 1 for poultry. Second, the Soviets produce much less feed grain than food grain, and they often have to feed valuable wheat to animals. Third, harvest fluctuations create serious problems in the management of livestock and, when there are feed shortfalls, livestock has to be slaughtered. This creates a temporary surplus of meat but, by reducing the livestock herds over the long run, domestic consumption is reduced for several years until the herds have been built up again. The Soviet authorities have been quick to import grain in bad crop years because the losses in livestock capital are sufficiently costly to make importing feed worthwhile, even if it has to be paid for in dollars. Some scholars have claimed that $1 spent for imported feed averts a loss of approximately $5 to $6 in livestock capital and future output of meat.

What can the Soviet Union do to increase agricultural output? It is unlikely that raising the rate of increase of factor inputs will help much. Difficulties in supplying increasing amounts of fertilizer, plus diminishing returns on that input, are not encouraging. Furthermore, the enormous proportion of the nation's annual capital investment already going to agriculture, combined with the low rate of return on such investments, makes a further significant increase in investments unlikely. Finally, given the country's labor shortage and the lack of amenities in rural areas, it seems reasonable to predict a continuation of the steady net outflow of young workers from agriculture.

Self-Sufficiency: Elusive Goal

The situation might be improved by allowing peasants working on collective and state farms to have larger private plots. (Presumably, it would be politically impossible to change over completely to private-enterprise agriculture.) Private plots occupy just 3 percent of the land but produce approximately one fifth of the nation's crops and about one third of its livestock products. Why not turn the peasants loose on even larger plots? The problem is that the peasants work their little plots very intensively. To cultivate still larger plots, it might be necessary for them to reduce substantially the time they put in on collective and state farms. This would be difficult to allow, given the steadily declining size and quality of the agricultural work force.

The only remaining possibility for raising output would seem to lie in increasing agricultural efficiency and thereby raising total productivity. Western scholars have often pointed to the low level of Soviet agrotechnology as an important reason for poor performance. Much could be done by using better breeds of livestock, improved varieties of crops, advanced cultivation prac-

Langley in *The Christian Science Monitor* © 1982 TCSPS

"You can help by staying down on the farm and working hard."

tices and the like. But this has been known for years, and progress has been slow—as it has in other sectors where a shift from extensive to intensive methods has long been in order.

One final point: the U.S.S.R., like many other East European nations, heavily subsidizes agriculture, with the consequence that food prices are lower than they otherwise would be. This, of course, encourages demand for food and, under present conditions, creates additional dissatisfaction by increasing the gap between demand and supply. That prices have been raised so little in the U.S.S.R. is probably due to the political risks such a policy entails. The recent Polish experience will undoubtedly deter Soviet planners from reducing or eliminating food subsidies.

All in all, the prospects for agriculture do not appear bright, and it is not clear what the Soviets can do to change them. The new Food Program announced in May 1982 does not appear promising. As in the past, the government is promising small increases in investment, supplies to agriculture, and incentives, as well as improvements in rural living and working conditions. In a peaceful world, the U.S.S.R. would probably have abandoned the goal of being agriculturally self-sufficient long ago. Instead, it would have relied on imports for a significant portion of its domestic needs. But given the current political climate, it seems clear that the Soviets will continue to strive for as much agricultural self-sufficiency as possible and accept all the negative consequences that such a strategy entails.

PETROLEUM

The Soviet Union, like the industrialized Western nations, is dependent on petroleum for economic growth. Unlike other advanced nations, however, the U.S.S.R. faces qualitatively different petroleum prospects. After all, it is the world's largest producer of petroleum and exports about one fourth of its output, second in value only to Saudi Arabia. About half of its exports are sold to the West for hard currency, the other half to Eastern Europe. Petroleum and petroleum-product exports have accounted for half of the U.S.S.R.'s hard currency earnings from commercial sources in the past few years and have therefore been of enormous importance. However, although total Soviet energy exports have grown at about 10 percent a year over the past 20 years, it is unlikely that the trend in petroleum can be maintained.

Until recently, Soviet petroleum output increased by leaps and bounds: from 30 million metric tons in 1950 to 350 million in 1970 to 603 million in 1980. In 1981, output rose by only 1 percent—to 609 million tons. The recent slowdown is highlighted by the fact that the Soviet five-year target for 1985 is only 620 million to 645 million metric tons, virtually the same as the 1980 target, which was not achieved.

For most of the postwar period, growth of output had been centered in the Urals-Volga region, which replaced the Baku-Grozny fields that dominated prewar output. In the late sixties and seventies, as output in the Urals-Volga region topped out, rich new fields in western Siberia began to pick up the slack, in particular the giant Samotlor field in the Tyumen region, which produced almost 150 million tons. Samotlor now appears to have peaked, and for the first time in the postwar period there do not appear to be any large fields to take its place.

Soviet petroleum output problems were dramatically highlighted in 1977. That year the CIA predicted not only that Soviet and East European demand would outrun Soviet supply, but that Soviet output would peak around 1980, decline thereafter for most of the decade and that, by 1985 or so, the U.S.S.R. would enter the petroleum market as a net importer. More recently, in a revised estimate, the CIA sees output declining more slowly and the U.S.S.R. not becoming a net importer until close to 1990. Significantly, no other forecast has been this pessimistic, and other experts differ substantially in their predictions.

What can be said with certainty, in any case, is that the wide divergence of existing estimates reflects the short-run uncertainties in the Soviet petroleum picture. Nevertheless, even the most recent official Soviet estimate projects a rate of growth that most Western experts feel will not keep up with expected domestic requirements.

Production Down

What are some of the factors underlying the more pessimistic estimates of Soviet petroleum production? As noted earlier, there do not appear to be any giant fields to replace Samotlor in the next decade. Of course, others may be found eventually—if not in western Siberia, then in eastern Siberia. However, if new petroleum activity is located in eastern Siberia, extraction and transportation costs are going to be a lot higher. Conditions in eastern Siberia are much harsher: the region lacks infrastructure and is much farther from consumption centers.

Moreover, the Soviet technique of accelerating the flow of oil by injecting pressurized water into the reservoirs has begun to backfire. While this minimized the number of wells that had to be dug and increased flows in the early stages, more recently the pumps have been removing as much water as oil from the ground. And that means less oil, a need for more pumps and new wells, and lower productivity.

Another indicator has been the fact that recent exploratory drilling has increased output only by 40 percent of that achieved by comparable levels of drilling ten years earlier. Further, much of the exploratory drilling has been for new wells in old areas rather than for new wells in new areas like eastern Siberia where a find would be much more likely to uncover a new giant. Nor have the Russians been able to produce high-quality drill bits and advanced seismic technology. Not only do their drill bits wear out quickly, but they cannot be used to the same depth as American bits. Lack of first-class seismic technology has also handicapped the search for new fields.

Foreign Technology and Conservation

On the positive side, many Soviet difficulties can be partly or fully overcome by importing foreign technology. Between 1971 and 1976, for example, the U.S.S.R. imported $3 billion worth of oil and gas equipment and $4 billion worth of steel pipe. Although the United States has placed an embargo on exports of some equipment, the Soviets have been able to purchase adequate substitutes for most of the embargoed products. Most Western observers feel that it is just a matter of time before the Soviets catch up technologically and find large new sources of petroleum. Even the CIA predicts a rise in output again in the 1990s.

Another potentially positive factor is that, as of 1982, the Soviets do not yet appear to have made much effort at conservation. Soviet conservation efforts will, of course, have to be concentrated on industry, since they have far fewer automobiles than most Western nations. Although there seems to be plenty of room for conservation, it is questionable whether the poor incentive structure in Soviet industry will allow conservation measures to work. Ironically, the projected slowdown in overall economic growth may also contribute to energy conservation, since slower growth reduces the demand for petroleum.

Finally, it is to the Soviets' advantage that their output of natural gas is rising rapidly and to some extent substitutes for petroleum at home and as a hard currency export abroad. In fact, the U.S.S.R. should eventually become the largest producer of natural gas in the world. The much publicized Urengoi-Yamburg pipeline is one major channel for converting this expanding output into hard currency earnings.

Another related issue needs to be touched upon. Would a future oil shortage motivate the U.S.S.R. to attempt a forceful expansion into the Middle East? According to some analysts, the Soviet invasion of Afghanistan points in this direction. On the other hand, a good argument can be made that the probability of such expansion is very low. The Soviet leaders must be aware that any military threat to U.S. and NATO oil supplies could provoke military retaliation and start a war. The Soviets are, therefore, unlikely to engage in such a high-risk action.

Soviet willingness to risk a war for petroleum also has to be considered in terms of potential economic gains. The U.S.S.R. probably faces, under the most pessimistic assumptions, a maximum annual petroleum import burden in today's prices of approximately $5 billion by 1985 and $15 billion by 1990. Even if an invasion of the Middle East enabled the U.S.S.R. to avoid costs of this magnitude—which are certainly on the high side—one would still have to weigh in the balance the costs of invasion and occupation. But would an occupation save the Soviets the cost of imported petroleum? It seems very unlikely. Only in the event that the captured nation were absorbed into the U.S.S.R. would it be possible to avoid a good part of the costs of importing the oil. And such a takeover seems most improbable. As long as the oil-exporting nation maintains its identity, the Soviets would have to keep paying for the oil. They might well receive preferential treatment, but even with preferential treatment, Soviet savings from occupation would be small. It seems more probable that, if forced to import petroleum in the 1980s—and that is a very big if—the U.S.S.R. will either enter the market and bid competitively for oil or attempt through diplomatic activity to get Western Europe to join it in guaranteeing oil deliveries.

THE POLISH CRISIS

That political influence over a country need not result in economic gains for the U.S.S.R. is most apparent from its trade relations with Eastern Europe. The U.S.S.R. supplies a good part of Eastern Europe's raw-material requirements (especially fuels) in return for machinery, equipment and other manufactured products. Over the past ten years, however, this exchange has become particularly unprofitable to the U.S.S.R. because the prices of raw materials, relative to the prices of machinery and equipment, have risen more rapidly in the world than in intra-Soviet-bloc trade. Thus, for example, in 1980 the Poles imported petroleum from the U.S.S.R. at approximately half the world price and exported railroad cars and fishing trawlers to the U.S.S.R. at 12 percent and 140 percent, respectively, above world prices. Nevertheless, despite its own petroleum difficulties, the Soviet Union has continued to supply Eastern Europe with petroleum and other raw materials below world prices, thereby forgoing very large profits. This implicit Soviet subsidy is estimated to have averaged $5.8 billion annually during 1974–78, $10.4 billion in 1979, and a staggering $21.7 billion in 1980. Moreover, the manufactured products the U.S.S.R. imports from Eastern Europe are generally inferior to those available in the West.

The Soviets were not always this sensitive to Eastern Europe's needs. Throughout much of the 1950s the U.S.S.R. literally exploited Eastern Europe by insisting on extremely unequal trade relations. It was only during the Khrushchev era that the picture changed and an attempt was made to use trade to enhance intrabloc political relationships. The U.S.S.R. stopped exploiting Eastern Europe and, in effect, accepted smaller economic gains, or even losses, in exchange for political goodwill.

In return for economic benefits, the bloc nations also reciprocate militarily and politically by allowing Soviet troops and weapons to be stationed in their territories; by supporting the U.S.S.R. in international forums; and by accepting Soviet political ideology, party domination and the like—in short by being quiescent allies.

Polish Crisis: Assessing the Costs

The burden of the Soviet Union's trade with Eastern Europe has been substantially increased by the Polish crisis of 1980-81. Poland has experienced the most severe economic decline of any developed nation in peacetime since the Great Depression 50 years ago. The economic crisis is, of course, as much a cause as an effect of a sociopolitical crisis, the most serious to have rocked Eastern Europe since Yugoslavia's defection from the Soviet bloc more than 30 years ago.

Indicative of the extent of Poland's economic problems is the fact that it is unable to pay even the current interest on its huge $27 billion foreign debt to the West. The severity of the decline is best reflected in official estimates and projections of the East European version of GNP—domestic net material product:

	1978	**1979**	**1980**	**1981 (July est.)**	**1982 (Plan)**
Annual Rate of Growth (%)	3.0	−2.3	−5.4	−14.5	−1.4[a]
Index (1978 = 100)	100.0	97.7	92.4	79.0	77.9[a]

[a]This official projection undoubtedly errs on the optimistic side.

Source: Z. Fallenbuchl, "Poland: A Way Out?" presented at the American Economic Association Meetings in Washington, D.C., December 29, 1981.

The Polish crisis adversely affects the Soviet as well as other East European economies in a number of ways:

1. Polish scheduled deliveries of many products (especially coal, sulfur, machinery and food) have been delayed or cancelled,

disrupting production in the importing nations. Polish coal exports to Eastern Europe, for example, reportedly dropped from 20 million tons in 1979 to 12 million in 1980 to an estimated 4 million in 1981. There is no end in sight to this problem.

2. The U.S.S.R., in particular, has been forced to provide Poland with relief in the form of commodities (especially crude oil, gas and iron ore) at low prices, as well as hard currency and unplanned ruble credits.

3. The Polish credit crisis, not to mention Rumania's impending credit crisis, will raise the cost and endanger the availability of future credits for all the Soviet-bloc nations. An explicit Polish default would make matters even worse.

4. Soviet support of the Polish military regime has stepped up the cold war, thereby endangering Western credits and exports of strategic commodities. Indeed, the United States has already imposed sanctions.

5. The crisis represents a military weakening of the Warsaw Pact's western front and could induce the U.S.S.R. to increase its military outlays.

6. The threatening example of Solidarity, Poland's free-trade-union movement, which was quashed in December 1981, might force the Soviet leadership to provide its own consumer sector with more goods than planned at the expense of investment and perhaps even military expenditures. In the short run, this could reduce the growth rate and worsen the hard currency balance of payments position.

It is almost impossible to quantify the drain on Soviet resources represented by the Polish crisis. One source speaks of $4 billion to $5 billion in Soviet assistance during the first year of crisis. Another puts Soviet direct financial aid at $2.15 billion. It has also been reported that the U.S.S.R. and Poland signed an $11.8 billion trade agreement (presumably for 1982) that includes $3.8 billion in new credits. In any case, it seems probable that the Polish crisis so far has drained about $5 billion annually from the Soviet economy. For a nation with an estimated $1.5 trillion GNP, this is not a lot—less than one half of 1 percent. And it would be even less of a problem if the Soviet economy were buoyant and growing as rapidly as it did in the 1950s. But under conditions of declining growth rates, the loss of perhaps one fifth of the annual increase in GNP in the form of assistance to Poland can be an unpleasant burden. While Soviet aid to Poland so far in 1982 seems to be down a bit from 1981 levels, the Polish crisis is by no means resolved, and no one knows what the future holds.

HARD CURRENCY BALANCE OF PAYMENTS AND TRADE

Although most Soviet trade has traditionally been with Eastern Europe, trade increased rapidly with Western Europe after 1960 and with the United States after 1970, thanks to détente. Between 1960 and 1980, Soviet trade with non-Communist countries grew from 27 percent of its total trade to 46 percent, of which trade with less-developed nations amounted to about 13 percent in 1980.

The Soviet Union began the 1970s with virtually no hard currency debt. Although it had trade deficits in the early seventies, these were offset, until 1974, by sales of gold and weapons. Large-scale foreign borrowing began in 1975–76, however, when Western recessions reduced Soviet exports at the same time that domestic harvest failures necessitated unprecedented increases in food imports. By the end of 1980, the Soviets had a gross debt of approximately $18 billion and a net debt of about $11 billion, the difference represented by Soviet financial assets in Western banks (see Table 4).

The Soviets appear to have acted fairly responsibly in the face of their growing debt. Total hard currency imports barely increased in 1976 and 1977 (see Table 1, page 20). And new equipment orders are estimated to have declined from $6 billion in 1976 to $3.8 billion in 1977 and to $2.8 billion in 1978.

At present, most observers deem the U.S.S.R. "creditworthy" and there has been no reluctance on the part of Western banks to extend additional loans at competitively low interest rates. As of 1978, its "debt-service ratio" (the percentage of export earnings required to finance debt repayment and interest) was 0.27 when measured against hard currency commodity export earnings and

Table 4
U.S.S.R.: Estimated Drawings, Scheduled Repayments on Western Credits, and Debt Outstanding
(in millions of U.S. dollars)

Since 1977, debt repayments have amounted to two thirds and interest payments one third of the total in column 2. The differences between gross and net debts outstanding are financial assets, such as deposits in Eurobanks, owned by the Soviets in the West.

	Estimated Drawings on Credits	Debt Repayments Plus Interest	Gross Debt Outstanding at End of Year	Net Debt Outstanding at End of Year
1971	511	358	1,803	582
1972	878	446	2,405	555
1973	1,737	729	3,745	1,166
1974	2,052	1,133	5,172	1,654
1975	6,371	1,773	10,574	7,451
1976	5,661	2,398	14,849	10,115
1977	2,850	3,115	15,724	11,230
1978	3,051	3,571	16,423	11,217
1979	3,660	4,230	17,283	—
1980	3,576	4,675	17,809	—

Sources: First three columns: CIA, *Handbook of Economic Statistics*, 1979, p. 68; 1981, p. 63. Last column: Ericson and Miller, *op. cit.*, p. 224.

only 0.18 against total hard currency earnings. These quite respectable ratios, by today's standards, had fallen to 0.20 and 0.16 respectively by 1980. The Soviet performance stands in sharp contrast with that of other members of the bloc, who have high debt-service ratios and are therefore viewed as serious credit risks.

The Soviet balance-of-payments situation in the 1980s, however, is likely to deteriorate due to the Polish crisis, rising imports of grain, and declining exports of petroleum.

As previously noted, Poland may already have become a hard currency drain on the Soviets. For one thing, Poland has apparently received hard currency loans and will probably receive more. For another, to the extent that the U.S.S.R. has to render unexpected commodity assistance to the Poles, either it may have to replace some of these products with unplanned purchases in hard currency markets or, in cases like petroleum, it may have to divert exports away from hard currency buyers.

Furthermore, the need to allocate hard currency reserves to imports of grain will increasingly be a matter for Soviet concern. Most experts expect the quantity of grain imported to rise slowly over the coming years. In value terms, however, the increase will be even more rapid because of projected increases in grain prices. In August 1982 the U.S.S.R. signed the second one-year extension of its agreement to import 6 million to 8 million tons of U.S. grain.

The most serious balance-of-payments threat concerns petroleum. Petroleum exports provided approximately half of total hard currency earnings in the late 1970s, reaching a high of $14 billion in 1980. But, as noted earlier, the future of these exports is problematical. The most optimistic plausible forecast for 1985 projects maintenance of the current level of petroleum exports only if conservation is very successful. Given the nature of the planning-incentive system in the U.S.S.R., however, the likelihood of getting managers to implement effectively oil conservation measures seems slim. Moreover, in the likely event that conservation efforts fail to yield dramatic results, then hard currency exports are bound to decline.

What, if any, are the extenuating circumstances? And what can the Soviets do to improve their hard currency position in the 1980s?

On the plus side are the prospective increased earnings from sales of natural gas. The U.S.S.R. has the largest natural gas reserves in the world, and it is developing them rapidly. Hard currency earnings from natural gas increased twelvefold between 1975 and 1980, exceeding $3 billion in the latter year. In fact, future hard currency earnings from sales of natural gas should be at least large enough to offset projected increases in the costs of importing grain. When the Urengoi-Yamburg gas pipeline goes into operation, the hard currency earnings from gas exports are expected to total $10 billion annually.

The Soviets can also divert more petroleum for export by increasing their output and consumption of coal. However, prospects for doing so are not promising because the Soviets have so far fallen way behind their targeted production.

Another option available to the Soviets is to reduce petroleum and other potential hard currency exports to Eastern Europe and divert them either to domestic needs or to the West. Some relief will undoubtedly be sought along these channels, but probably not much will be gained, since there are obvious limits to this alternative. Anything more than minor cutbacks in Soviet exports could have a serious impact on the political and military cohesion of the bloc, particularly in the wake of the Polish crisis. Furthermore, any significant weakening of the East European economies would also have a negative impact on the Soviet economy.

Another possible solution is to reduce overall East-West trade and to increase intrabloc trade. Efforts toward greater economic integration are already apparent in the Soviet bloc's Comprehensive Program of 1971–75 and the Coordinated Plan for Multilateral Integration of 1976–80. For systemic reasons these efforts have not been too successful, except in fairly obvious activities such as jointly financed and constructed oil and gas pipelines and the Soviet-East European electricity grid. However, East-West problems will insure that attempts at further intrabloc trade and integration continue.

The U.S.S.R. can minimize its losses from reduced Western imports by concentrating these reductions in low-gain sectors. There appears to have been a considerable number of low-gain products and projects among Soviet imports in the past and probably at present. For example, about one third of all Soviet beer is produced in breweries built by foreign contractors; a large percentage of Soviet sugar beets is processed by imported equipment; the West Germans built a steel mill in Kursk; the Japanese helped to open and operate a coal mine in Yakutia; the Soviets imported welding equipment from the United States while selling more advanced welding equipment to an American consortium. These transactions may be quite rational and advantageous under ordinary conditions, but as hard currency becomes scarce, it will undoubtedly be reserved for transactions that provide larger gains.

'Compensation Agreements'

The Soviets could make more extensive use of "compensation agreements" with Western enterprises. Under such agreements, the Soviets pay for equipment with the output eventually produced by that equipment. For example, they pay for pipe with future shipments of natural gas via the projected pipeline. These agreements provide not only relatively cheap credit but also what are, in effect, guaranteed hard currency markets. A related type of transaction is the "counterpurchase" deal, in which exports and imports are exchanged simultaneously. One of the largest of these barter deals involved the Occidental Petroleum Company, an American company, which exchanged U.S. superphosphoric acid for Soviet ammonia, potash and urea.

In aggregate, how large are the compensation deals? One expert predicts that hard currency exports based on such agreements will rise from $2 billion in 1980 to $4 billion in 1985. This is not a very large figure—but it could represent a sizable part of Soviet hard currency earnings if the balance of payments deteriorates sharply.

While the Soviets are anxious to complete more compensation agreements, it is not clear how successful they will be. Such agreements are usually not optimal for the Western partner, who assumes greater than average risks. For example, products may be ready for repayment after the market has become saturated. A further problem is dealing with the impenetrable Soviet bureaucracy and with the Soviet reluctance to have foreigners on their soil for any length of time. In addition, many entrepreneurs, and especially the Japanese, have found the Chinese to be better partners.

Special Export Industries?

The Soviets are also considering the idea of establishing special export enterprises with the kind of preferential treatment now assigned their weapons production sector. Establishment of priority conditions and special privileges for the enterprises involved, insistence on quality output, as well as intimate ties between those enterprises and research and development institutes, could result

Table 5
U.S.S.R.: Average Annual Rates of Growth of Total GNP Production, Inputs and Productivity, 1951-80
(in percentages)

GNP—or the total output of goods and services of a nation—grows when either the quantity of inputs or the productivity of those inputs grows. Productivity increases as a result of changes in skills, technology, organization, climate, and so forth. In comparison with most advanced Western nations, Soviet growth has been relatively more dependent on increases in quantities of inputs than on increases in productivity.

Technical note: **While the increase in output is equal to the simple sum of the increases in inputs and productivity (except for rounding), the totals of inputs and of factor productivities are not equal to the simple sums of their individual parts in the table because the parts are weighted differently, according to their importance.**

	1951-55	1956-60	1961-65	1966-70	1971-75	1976-80
Total GNP	6.0	5.8	5.0	5.5	3.8	2.7
Inputs:						
Labor (man-hours), capital and land	4.5	3.9	4.1	3.9	4.1	3.6
Man-hours	1.9	.6	1.6	2.0	1.9	1.4
Capital	9.0	9.8	8.7	7.5	7.9	6.9
Land	4.0	1.3	.6	−.3	.9	0
Factor productivity:						
Labor (man-hours), capital and land	1.4	1.8	.9	1.5	−.2	−.8
Man-hours	4.6	5.1	3.4	3.4	1.8	1.3
Capital	−2.7	−3.6	−3.3	−1.9	−3.8	−3.9
Land	1.9	4.4	4.4	5.8	2.9	2.8

Sources: For 1950-75, Rush V. Greenslade, "The Real Gross National Product of the U.S.S.R., 1950-75," in *Soviet Economy in a New Perspective,* 1st ed., Joint Economic Committee, U.S. Congress, Washington, D.C., USGPO, 1976, p. 279; for 1976–80, CIA *Handbook of Economic Statistics,* 1981, p. 60.

in quality products capable of competing in Western markets. On the other hand, introducing a special export sector would increase the burden on the overall civilian sector and might also siphon resources from the military sector. In view of the current troubles in the civilian sector and of the sanctity of the military, it might be very difficult to implement a priority export sector of sufficient magnitude and efficiency to have a discernible impact.

If some of the more pessimistic scenarios regarding petroleum and climate come to pass, the U.S.S.R.'s hard currency balance of payments will deteriorate, and the authorities will be forced to borrow more heavily and to curb imports. To make matters worse, most of the ameliorative measures that have been suggested are unlikely to have a significant effect.

Table 6
Gross Investment as Percentage of GNP
(at factor cost)

These figures show how, between 1960 and 1980, in an effort to stem the decline of growth, the share of GNP devoted to increasing the capital stock of the nation increased from one fourth to one third of total output produced. A rate of investment of 33 percent of GNP is very high, higher than that of any major industrial nation with the exception of Japan.

1960	1965	1970	1975	1976	1977	1978	1979	1980
24	27	28	31	32	32	32	32	33

Source: CIA, *Handbook of Economic Statistics,* 1981, p. 56.

TECHNOLOGY

The more rapid introduction of new technology into Soviet production processes can contribute greatly to solving its growth problems. As noted earlier, Soviet growth in the past has owed more to increases in the quantity of labor and especially of capital than to changes in their quality (see Tables 5 and 6). Given sharply diminishing returns on capital, as well as reduced annual increments to the labor force and to capital stock, the Soviets must shift from extensive to intensive growth, which means, primarily, speeding up the introduction and diffusion of new technology. New technology, by increasing capital productivity, offsets diminishing returns.

There are two ways of accelerating introduction of new technology. One is by initiating economic reforms that provide the proper incentives for technological innovation. (The 1973 Production Association Reform was an attempt along these lines that was not, apparently, very successful.) The other is to continue importing new technology.

Since the late 1960s, the Soviets have substantially expanded purchases of machinery and equipment from the West, some of it relatively advanced technologically. While this imported technology has undoubtedly had some positive effect on the economy, it has not been able to stem the downward trend in rate of growth for several reasons. As suggested earlier, the Soviet industrial economy does not provide fertile soil for planting the seeds of new technology. It is difficult to get a plant manager to introduce new methods of production and just as difficult to disseminate the technology to other enterprises. Even when new technology is introduced, its advantages are often negated by the manner in which the new machinery and equipment are adapted to Soviet conditions. Several years ago, for example, the U.S.S.R. imported six chemical plants. These plants were originally designed to employ 91 auxiliary workers. In the Soviet adaptation of the plan, the number was expanded to 430. When the plants were finally in operation, 732 auxiliary workers were actually employed. As another example, in the early 1950s the U.S.S.R. introduced milking machines to replace milkmaids. In the mid-1970s this process was 95 percent completed—yet the number of milkmaids had declined only from 1 per 15 cows to 1 per 18 cows!

Soviet imports of advanced technology, moreover, have been too small to have a significant impact. In 1976 Soviet imports of all goods from all sources totaled approximately $38 billion, of which $12 billion was from the West, including $4 billion worth of machinery and equipment. (Of the $4 billion, only approximately one third represented advanced technology.) Moreover, the $4 billion figure amounted to only around 3 percent of total Soviet investment in machinery and equipment that year. The significance of these imports is reduced even further if they are measured against the total Soviet stock of machinery and equipment. Since that amounts to over $1 trillion, imports represent one third of 1 percent of the total valued in dollars. (Measured in domestic ruble prices, the above percentages would be somewhat higher.)

This does not mean that imports cannot make a large contribution in selected bottleneck areas, where the gains from breaking these bottlenecks may be many times the cost of the imports. Even if such gains should be five times that realized from normal investment, however, the volume of such imports would still be too small to have a major impact on overall economic growth.

To sum up, for a breakthrough on the technology front to solve the Soviet economic impasse, much larger imports of new technology or radical economic reform is required.

ECONOMIC REFORM

In the past quarter century, the Soviets have instituted four major reforms whose impact on economic performance appears to have been minimal (although it is probably too early to evaluate the impact of the 1979 reform). All four reforms accepted central planning by direct controls, while trying to make it work better. Since central planning is, itself, the major cause of the U.S.S.R.'s difficulties, administrative tinkering was bound to fail.

Of course, even fundamental reforms need not significantly improve Soviet performance. Hungary's New Economic Mechanism introduced in 1968, which abandoned rigid central planning and gave a freer hand to state enterprises, appears to have led to an improvement in product quality, but does not appear to have increased Hungary's rate of growth above that of other East European nations. Nevertheless, the Soviet economic performance would undoubtedly improve if the U.S.S.R. shifted to a modified form of market socialism under which plant managers had some autonomy over output and prices, competition existed, prices became more meaningful, profits and not output or sales became the criterion of management success, and overfull employment planning was eliminated.

However, there are several reasons for believing that a radical reform would be opposed by almost everyone in the production hierarchy. The bulk of the management and planning bureaucracy would stand to lose their jobs if the market replaced central planning. Production association and plant management personnel would feel threatened by the sharp change in the nature of their work: instead of being told how much to produce, where to ship their output and where to buy their inputs, they would have to rely on their own wits and compete for inputs and for sales of outputs. Workers would also be opposed to decentralization, viewing it as a threat to their job security.

There is also evidence that most Soviet economists and political leaders still believe in the superiority of central planning over the market, partly for ideological reasons and partly because of the very poor performances, in recent years, of most of the advanced Western industrial nations.

A radical economic reform could also have dangerous political repercussions. The abortive Czech reform of 1968 demonstrated the very close relationship between economic change and political and intellectual liberalization.

A Soviet radical reform would also undoubtedly lead to similar reforms in Eastern Europe. As a result, Eastern Europe's foreign trade would probably be conducted on the basis of market criteria, East-West trade would rapidly increase at the expense of intra-bloc trade, and the bloc itself would cease to be a tightly knit trading group. Since the political consequences of increased economic ties with the West would be even more dangerous, Soviet leaders would surely be unwilling to countenance reforms whose consequence would be a weakening of their system of satellites.

For these reasons, it appears unlikely that the Soviet Union will adopt radical reforms in the near future, except in the improbable event of an acute economic crisis. (It is worth noting, nevertheless, that over the past year some Soviet leaders have referred to the Hungarian New Economic Mechanism in nonpejorative terms.) At the moment, however, Soviet difficulties appear only mildly disabling and chronic—not acute.

4

Prospects for the 1980s

Soviet economic prospects for the 1980s clearly are not good. The downward trend in the overall rate of growth will probably continue, while the rate of growth of the labor force declines and the economy fails to develop and diffuse new technology. Continued poor performance in agriculture, rising costs of extracting raw material and possible trouble with balance of payments will act as further drags. The costs of bailing out Poland and keeping up in the arms race may also be severe.

On the other hand, if the Soviets are lucky, the 1980s may turn out to be not much different from the 1970s when the U.S.S.R. did experience a respectable average rate of growth. A combination of better than average weather conditions for agriculture, achievement of the petroleum goals of the 1981-85 Five-Year Plan, and political and economic stability in Poland could result in perhaps a 3 to 4 percent annual GNP growth rate.

Even if pessimists prove to be correct, the Soviet predicament must be put in perspective. The U.S.S.R. is not alone in facing difficult economic and social problems. A Soviet economist writing a paper entitled "The United States Economy in the 1980s" would undoubtedly point to the following problems:

1. a low, and occasionally negative, overall rate of economic growth;
2. an alarmingly low rate of growth in productivity;
3. a steady decline in the rate of innovation and a low rate of investment;
4. a deteriorating position in world markets;
5. the precipitous decline of the automobile and steel industries, once the world leaders;
6. inability to control inflation without unacceptably high unemployment;
7. no rise in workers' real wages and the highest unemployment in 40 years;
8. the wholesale dismantling of social welfare programs in order to provide funds for a military buildup.

Indeed, the Soviet economist might even conclude that the U.S. economy is on the verge of collapse.

Foreign Economic Policy Implications

In the aftermath of World War II, U.S. economic policies toward the U.S.S.R. reflected the fact that the U.S.S.R. had become this country's major political and military rival. Trade and credit relations between the two countries virtually ceased. U.S. exporters were not allowed to sell anything that might provide the U.S.S.R. with military, military-related, or large economic benefits. The United States pressed its West European allies to take similar actions. The U.S.S.R. was also denied most-favored-nation status in trade, so that its exports to the United States had to hurdle much higher tariffs than the same products from non-Communist nations. Medium- and long-term credits were also on the proscribed list. Most of the sanctions against the U.S.S.R. were applied to Soviet allies in Eastern Europe as well.

While U.S. sanctions may have slowed Soviet development, they can hardly be termed very successful, for it was in this early postwar period that the Soviet Union (and Eastern Europe) experienced its most rapid rates of economic growth, not to mention success in the development of atomic weapons, missiles and space technology. Why weren't U.S. sanctions more effective? There are a number of reasons. The period until the early 1960s was characterized by Soviet extensive growth requiring a maximum of mobilization of domestic resources and a minimum of assistance from abroad. Soviet scientists made large strides in nuclear weapons and rocketry, with the help of East German scientists and some espionage, and our NATO allies were much less enthusiastic than we were in applying restrictive controls on trade with the bloc.

In keeping with détente in the late 1960s, the Nixon Administration tried to relax trade restrictions with the U.S.S.R. in return for Soviet concessions on the first strategic arms limitation treaty (SALT I). But the Administration was thwarted, in part, by congressional passage in 1974 of the much-publicized Jackson-Vanik Amendment, which tied U.S. trade concessions to Soviet liberalization of their emigration policy, a form of linkage the Soviets rejected. Nevertheless, U.S. export control policy was substantially liberalized in the 1970s, though not by as much as our European allies' policies. Toward the end of the seventies, however, in response to Soviet human rights violations, the Carter Administration tightened up U.S. trade policy, including export controls. The Soviet invasion of Afghanistan and the military crackdown in Poland put economic relations between the United States and the Soviet Union back on a virtual cold-war footing.

Attempts to pressure our NATO allies into joining the United States in cold-war economic policies toward the U.S.S.R. have not been successful. For this past year, a battle has raged over the Siberian gas pipeline. The West European allies have refused to withdraw from the pipeline deal, and the Reagan Administration has begun to take punitive measures against not only the foreign subsidiaries of U.S. firms but also foreign firms—British, French, Italian and West German—that are participating in the construction of the pipeline, and thereby has weakened the NATO alliance.

In some respects, the U.S.S.R. and the East European countries are more susceptible to U.S. pressure now than they were in the fifties and early sixties. In contrast to this earlier period, most

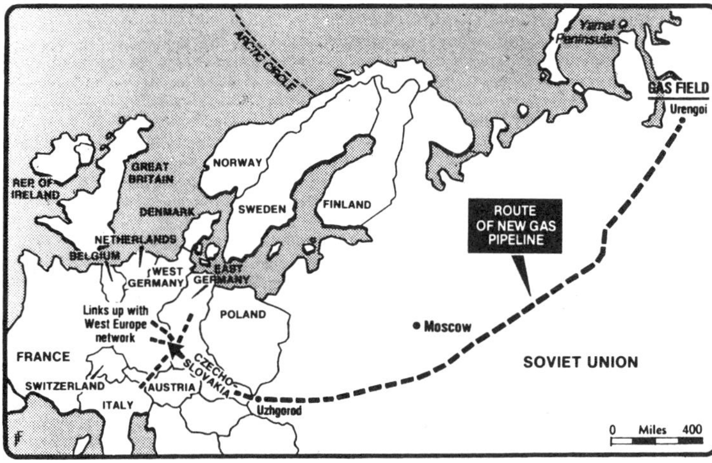

Reprinted by permission from *The Christian Science Monitor* © 1982 TCSPS

Projected route of the Soviet gas pipeline.

East European economies are now faltering and in need of imported technology and the hard currency to pay for it. However, the United States is in a much less advantageous position to exploit this leverage. The United States is no longer as dominant an economic power as it was 20 or 30 years ago; nor is it the only military superpower. Without extensive economic ties with the Soviet Union, the United States is in a weak position to hurt it by reducing or eliminating trade. Moreover, U.S. leverage is greatly reduced by West European unwillingness to join in applying economic sanctions.

This last fact is of sufficient importance to merit closer attention. Both the Carter and Reagan Administrations have worked hard, and failed, to develop a Western consensus on sanctions. Their lack of success is not difficult to understand. Western and Eastern Europe currently enjoy much closer ties than ever before in terms of exports, imports and credits. Western Europe relies on Eastern Europe for part of its requirements of raw materials and energy and depends on East European importers to buy a good percentage of its exports of manufactured products. For example, the percentage of West Germany's labor force engaged in producing exports for Eastern Europe is eight times that of the United States. And when the Siberian pipeline is completed by the late 1980s, France, West Germany and Italy will be getting about one third of their natural gas supplies from the Soviet Union, which, in turn, will be earning an estimated $10 billion annually in hard currency payments. Moreover, most of that $10 billion will be spent in Western Europe. So, to ask Western Europe to give up trade with Eastern Europe is asking a lot. Besides, the United States set a poor example when President Ronald Reagan, early in his Administration, removed controls from grain exports to the U.S.S.R.—the only sizable U.S. export to the nation—for purely domestic political considerations.

Once the pipeline is completed, East-West interdependence will increase. The fact that the Soviets will be earning hard currency with which to buy technology, beef up their military and finance their Cuban, Vietnamese and other third-world friends is one cause for worry on the part of the United States. Another cause for U.S. concern is that the Soviets may gain political leverage over Western Europe. The West Europeans have attempted to ease those concerns by pointing out that Soviet gas will be only 5 percent of Europe's total energy supplies. Further, they contend that in a crisis they could help one another with various forms of energy cooperation—for example, a European grid system permitting the sharing of energy—and thereby prevent the Soviets from using the threat of supply cutoffs as a means of blackmail. Finally, imports of gas will be partly matched by reduced imports of Soviet oil.

In the long run, the arguments for aborting the pipeline project do not appear very compelling. The world does, in fact, face an energy-short future. Western Europe will have to import a large part of its energy from the U.S.S.R. or the Middle East or both, and, in light of the Middle East's chronic instability, it is not at all clear that it can be viewed as a more reliable supplier than the Soviet Union. In any event, not putting all the eggs in one risky basket is certainly a rational strategy and explains why Western Europe decided to go ahead with the Siberian gas project.

Western Europe's clear intention of pursuing trade with the Soviet bloc poses problems for U.S. export control policies. To the extent that this nation enforces controls which are rendered ineffective by its allies, the alliance is bound to suffer. Frictions develop as a result of U.S. pressures on the other NATO nations to conform to American export-control standards. The controls also create domestic problems. American exporters feel cheated when they see that the effect of U.S. efforts is not to deprive the U.S.S.R. of desired imports but to shift the exports and profits to competitors in Western Europe and Japan. In short, U.S. export policies are ineffective, divisive and, therefore, perhaps more damaging to the United States than to the U.S.S.R. Even if NATO cooperated fully with U.S. export policies, the damage to the Soviet economy would probably be insufficient to tilt Soviet policies in the desired direction. This makes the case for restrictive policies appear all the weaker.

There remain, however, two possible reasons for restrictive controls on exports to the U.S.S.R. First, the United States may feel that, as a matter of principle, it must react strongly to such events as the Soviet invasion of Afghanistan and the imposition by the Polish military government of martial law in Poland. The Export Administration Act of 1979 specifically provides for export controls for foreign policy as well as security reasons. Although applying such controls, even when they are not likely to have much effect, may appear quixotic to some, deeds do after all speak louder than words. Second, Soviet attainment of rough military parity with the United States makes it very important that the United States control exports of militarily useful technology to the U.S.S.R. To the extent that these technologies are shared by some of its NATO allies, then every argument should be brought to bear on them to impose parallel controls in those instances in which there has been disagreement. This having been said, it is nonetheless probably fair to note that there has often been a tendency in this country to apply controls more broadly than required by U.S. security interests.

As with export controls, the United States applies much more restrictive lending policies toward the U.S.S.R. and Eastern

Europe than do its NATO partners. Poland's de facto default on its debts, along with the very serious credit difficulties faced by several other East European nations, has given the United States an opportunity to pressure Western Europe into applying more restrictive credit policies to the Soviet bloc. Indeed, some members of the Reagan Administration would like the United States and Western Europe to declare Poland legally in default on its debts and thereby make it harder and more expensive for the U.S.S.R. and Eastern Europe to get new loans. The basic U.S. motive is not, of course, to hurt Eastern Europe but to hurt the Soviet Union by weakening Eastern Europe and forcing the Soviets to divert resources to its assistance. In this manner, Poland's neighbors—like Poland itself—would become a drain on the Soviet economy.

But is it really in the U.S. interest to try to get Western Europe to limit credits to the East below an amount dictated by a prudent lending policy, or to have Poland or other East European nations declared in default? One problem with the "hard-line" approach is that West Europeans will refuse to apply overrestrictive credit policies, which would result in huge financial losses owing to reduced trade and the elimination of the massive East European debts. Defaulting Poland would save that nation the trouble of servicing a debt of approximately $27 billion. Unnecessarily restricting credit to Rumania, East Germany and Hungary could send these nations into downward spirals that might spell similar defaults, thereby raising the ante to well over $50 billion. Defaults of this magnitude could cause a serious Western financial crisis. The other problem with this approach is that it would negatively influence Western strategic interests by driving the East Europeans into Soviet arms at a time when many of these nations would prefer to move in the other direction.

What, then, is the United States to do? Clearly, the way for the United States to proceed is to seek policy coordination with West European nations, industries and banks in the realization that U.S. efforts alone are unlikely to be either effective or productive. West Europeans have too much to lose economically to go along with a U.S. policy that would damage their interests and sharpen the East-West confrontation without significantly improving the West's military position. A jointly conceived United States-West European policy may be less than what the United States might want, but at least it will produce results. And results, after all, are the point of policy in the first place.

Talking It Over

A Note for Students and Discussion Groups

This pamphlet, like its predecessors in the HEADLINE SERIES, is published for every serious reader, specialized or not, who takes an interest in the subject. Many of our readers will be in classrooms, seminars or community discussion groups. Particularly with them in mind, we present below some discussion questions—suggested as a starting point only—and references for further reading.

Discussion Questions

The Reagan Administration has been operating on the assumption that the U.S.S.R. cannot afford an arms race with the United States. Do you agree or disagree? Why?

To what factors do you attribute the Soviet economic slowdown in the sixties and seventies? Are any of these factors responsible for the stagflation experienced by the advanced Western nations? In what respects do the Communist and capitalist difficulties experienced recently differ from each other?

Why is it that the quality of most products manufactured for the civilian sector in the U.S.S.R. is below Western standards whereas the quality of military and space hardware ranks high?

The Reagan Administration is opposed to the West European-Soviet natural gas pipeline. Why? Evaluate the U.S. position on both economic and political grounds.

What measures were introduced by Stalin in the late twenties and early thirties that might be considered responsible for the rapid rate of growth in the prewar period? Why aren't these same factors applied to speed up growth today?

The Soviets are the largest producers of petroleum in the world and have the largest coal and gas reserves in the world. Yet they seem to have energy problems. Discuss.

READING LIST

Bergson, Abram, *The Economics of Soviet Planning.* Brooklyn, N.Y., Greenwood House, 1980 (reprint of 1964 ed.). The first major monograph on Soviet central planning by the leading scholar in the field. Although it was written before the reforms of 1965, 1973 and 1979, it remains very relevant.

——, *Productivity and the Social System: The U.S.S.R. and the West.* Cambridge, Mass., Harvard University Press, 1978. A very good collection of articles comparing the economic performance of the U.S.S.R. with that of advanced Western nations.

——, and Levine, Herbert, eds., *The Soviet Economy Toward the Year 2000.* Winchester, Mass., Allen & Unwin, 1982. The results of the proceedings of a conference held in 1980 in which leading scholars in the various fields (covered in this pamphlet) wrote lengthy essays on their specialties. It will undoubtedly be the major reference work on the long-run outlook for the U.S.S.R. for at least the next five to ten years.

Berliner, Joseph S., *Innovation Decision in Soviet Industry.* Cambridge, Mass., MIT Press, 1976. Definitive study of Soviet practices and problems relating to innovation and technology.

Ellman, Michael, *Socialist Planning.* New York, Cambridge University Press, 1979. An up-to-date study of central planning, somewhat more technical than Bergson's study.

Gregory, Paul, and Stuart, Robert, *Soviet Economic Structure and Performance,* 2nd ed. New York, Harper and Row, 1981. Comprehensive textbook on the Soviet economy. Includes a chapter on the Czarist period.

Holzman, Franklyn D., "Are the Russians Really Outspending the U.S. on Defense?" *International Security,* Spring, 1980. An elaboration of the author's view that the CIA's estimates overstate Soviet defense expenditures relative to those of the U.S.

——, *International Trade Under Communism: Politics and Economics.* New York, Basic Books, 1976. An introductory text that lays out the principles of trade under central planning and contains historical chapters on intrabloc trade, East-West trade, and trade between the Communist and less-developed nations.

Kahan, Arcadius, and Ruble, Blair A., eds., *Industrial Labor in the U.S.S.R.* Elmsford, N.Y., Pergamon Press, 1979. A good up-to-date collection of articles on various aspects of the Soviet labor market.

Nove, Alec, *The Soviet Economic System.* Winchester, Mass., Allen & Unwin, 1977. An excellent introductory textbook by a British pioneer in the field of East European studies.

Richman, Barry, *Soviet Industrial Management.* Englewood Cliffs, N.J., Prentice-Hall, 1965. The most up-to-date monograph on the subject following Joseph Berliner's *Factory and Manager in the U.S.S.R.* (1957) and David Granick's *The Red Executive* (1960).

Soviet Economy in a Time of Change, 2 vols. Joint Economic Committee, U.S. Congress, Washington, D.C., U.S. Government Printing Office, 1979. A compendium of 58 recent articles by both academic and government economists, the best single source of information on almost every subject of current interest having to do with the Soviet economy.

Stuart, Robert C., *The Collective Farm in Soviet Agriculture.* Lexington, Mass., D.C. Heath, 1972. An excellent study of a most important Soviet institution.
